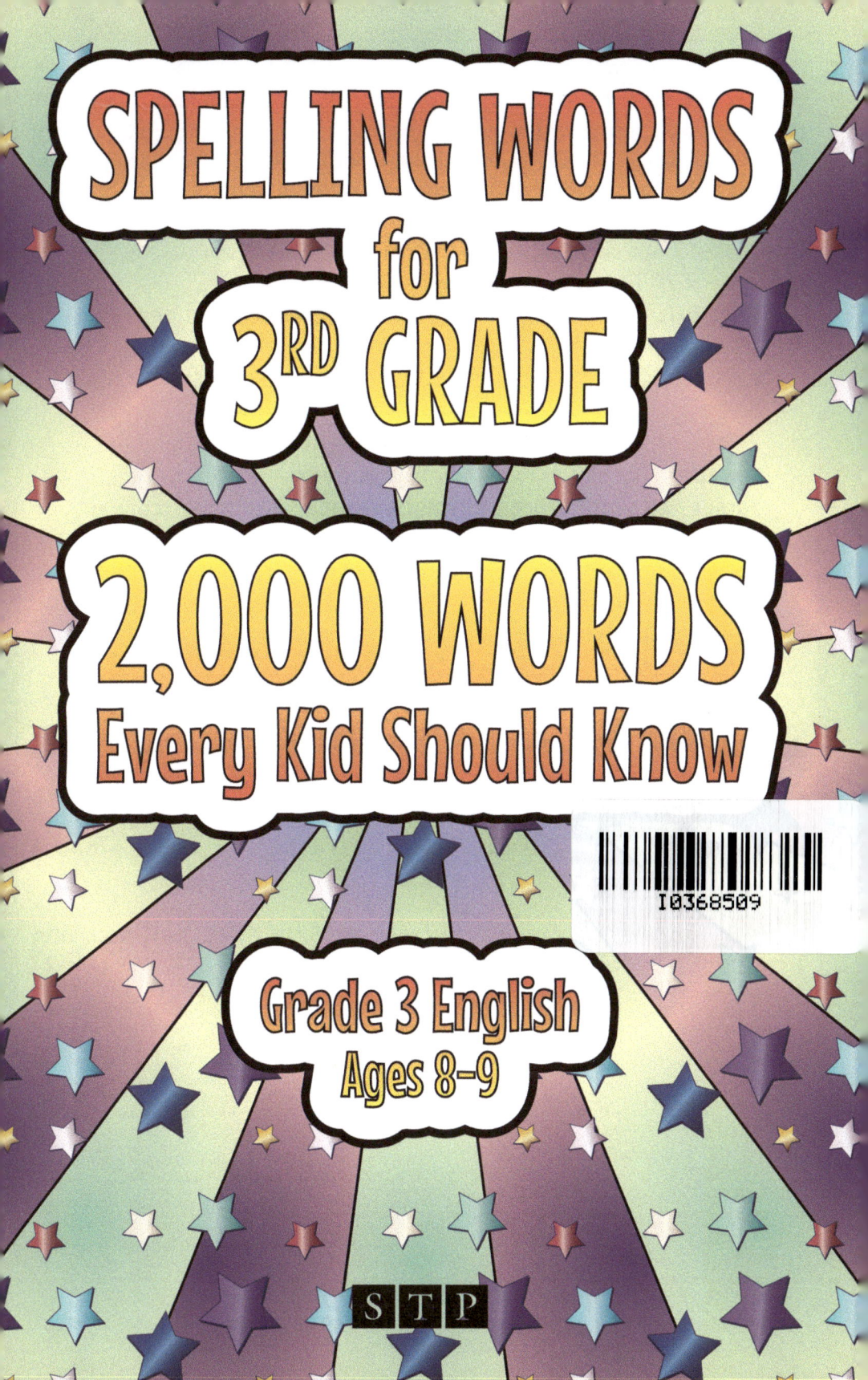

ABOUT THIS BOOK

Using a **fresh approach** to spellings lists, this illustrated collection of Spelling Words is designed **to make spelling fun** for children whilst helping them master essential spelling rules by the end of Grade 3.

Containing **2,000** carefully selected **level-appropriate** words, this book is made up of **70** Themed Spellings Lists that

- Have **brightly-colored illustrated backgrounds** and **engaging titles**
- Cover **loads of topics** that **actually interest children** such as Fourth of July, cities of the world, and board games
- Relate to other **areas covered at school** including marine creatures, ancient Rome, and healthy foods
- Target **key words that children overuse** (e.g. 'make', 'change', and 'real')
- Quietly introduce **specific areas of spelling** that children need to know (e.g. suffixes, homophones, doubling consonants, plural nouns, and silent letters)
- Are made up of **25 to 30 words each**

HOW TO USE IT

All the **lists are self-contained**, so you can work through them **in order**, or, you can dip in to use them for **focused practice**. And, as these lists are themed, they are **also a useful resource** for a range of **writing projects and exercises**.

For your convenience, an **Index** to the **spelling rules, patterns, and themed areas** dealt with by each of the lists is included at the **back of the book** on page 40.

Published by STP Books
An imprint of Swot Tots Publishing Ltd
124 City Road
London EC1V SNX

www.swottotspublishing.com

Text, design, illustrations and layout © Swot Tots Publishing Ltd
First published 2024

Swot Tots Publishing Ltd have asserted their moral right under the Copyright, Designs and Patents Act, 1988, to be identified as the author of this work.

All rights reserved. Without limiting the rights under copyright reserved above, no part of this publication may be reproduced, stored in a retrieval system, or transmitted in any form or by any means electronic, mechanical, photocopying, printing, recording, or otherwise without either the prior permission of the publishers or a license permitting restricted copying in the United Kingdom issued by the Copyright Licensing Agency Limited, 5th Floor, Shackleton House, Hay's Galleria, 4 Battle Bridge Lane, London SE1 2HX.

All other registered trademarks, products, and brand names are the property of their respective owners.

Typeset, cover design, and inside concept design by Swot Tots Publishing Ltd.

British Library Cataloguing-in-Publication Data. A catalogue record for this book is available from the British Library.

ISBN 978-1-912956-48-7

CONTENTS

Happy Endings I	5	Grrr-ammar!	14
That's Cheating!	5	Game On!	14
Silent, But Deadly I	6	Making It	15
Ring The Changes	6	Silent, But Deadly II	15
Mis- The Misled	7	As The Crow Flies	16
...Is A Person Who...	7	Happy Endings II	16
OW!!!!!	8	Fourth Of July	17
That Doesn't Look Right	8	Double Trouble?	17
T Is For Tiger &...	9	Tech Talk	18
Get Creative I	9	All Over The Place!	18
Business As U-su-AL	10	Perfect? Prefect?	19
Snap 'Em Up!	10	Farmers Market	19
Illegal To Irresponsible	11	Get Creative II	20
Chic 'Ch'	11	Kingly 'K'	20
King Arthur & Co.	12	C Is For Camel &...	21
Joining Forces	12	A...CHoo!	21
Ex Marks The Spot!	13	Hide & Seek!	22
On Your Feet!	13	Head-Scratchers	22

CONTENTS Cont.

Fine And Handy!	23	By Jupiter!	32
Happy Endings III	23	Clippety-Clop, Clippety-Clop	32
Sweet Tooth	24	Antihero Or Superstar?	33
Plague? Plaque?	24	Knock On Wood	33
Happy Days!	25	Happy Endings IV	34
Something Fishy	25	Chowin' Down	34
Oh My, Oh Y	26	It's All Make-Believe...	35
Glug, Glug, Glug	26	The Real Deal	35
Confounded Conjunctions	27	What A Ra-CK-et!	36
Written In The Stars	27	Heads First	36
What's A Person Who...	28	...Er	37
Silent, But Deadly III	28	D Is For Disaster	37
Where In The World...?	29	Write On!	38
Colorific!	29	Clouding Over	38
Are You Sure...Or Ture?	30	V..V.. VAMPIRES!	39
Full Of Beans!	30	That's A Proper Word?!	39
Sssss...	31		
Lots 'N Lots 'N Lots	31	Index	40

Happy Endings 1

angrily	lazily	giggly
busily	luckily	probably
cheerily	merrily	simply
clumsily	sleepily	sparkly
easily	steadily	squiggly
fussily	bubbly	terribly
greedily	crackly	wholly
happily	crumbly	wiggly
heavily	doubly	duly
hungrily	gently	truly

That's Cheating!

cheat	fake	mislead
con	falsify	misrepresent
cozen	fleece	misstate
crib	fudge	rip off
deceive	gull	shortchange
defraud	hoodwink	swindle
distort	hustle	take in
doctor	lead on	tamper with
double-cross	misguide	twist
dupe	misinform	warp

Silent, But Deadly I

high	align	gnome
bright	assign	gnu
fight	benign	phlegm
flight	malign	though
light	resign	through
sight	sign	
campaign	gnarled	
foreign	gnash	
reign	gnat	
sovereign	gnaw	

Ring The Changes

adapt	morph	remodel
adjust	mutate	replace
alter	recast	revamp
amend	rectify	revise
change	redo	rework
convert	refashion	shift
correct	refine	transfigure
emend	reform	transform
improve	rejig	upgrade
modify	remake	vary

Mis- The Misled

misadventure	misguided	misquote
misadvised	mishear	misread
misaligned	misinformed	misrule
misapplied	misinterpret	misshapen
misbehave	misjudge	misspell
misconduct	mislabel	mistake
misdeed	mislay	mistreat
misdiagnosis	misleading	mistrust
misdirect	mismatch	misunderstand
misfire	misplace	misuse

...Is A Person Who...

actor	governor	surveyor
administrator	inspector	survivor
commentator	instructor	traitor
conductor	inventor	translator
conqueror	investigator	tutor
constructor	legislator	
contractor	navigator	
decorator	sailor	
dictator	sculptor	
director	spectator	

Ow!!!!!

announced	doubt	mouse
bounce	encounter	pounce
boundary	foundation	roundabout
bounty	fountain	scoundrel
cloudy	hound	shroud
couch	loudest	slouch
countdown	lounge	soundless
countess	mound	spouse
countless	mount	thousand
county	mountains	warehouse

That Doesn't Look Right

accident	brought	popular
address	complete	protein
disappear	decide	purpose
embarrass	enough	receive
grammar	height	recipe
occur	heir	remember
successful	heist	strength
suppose	interest	theirs
tattoo	mention	thought
tomorrow	naughty	weird

T IS FOR TIGER &....

tapir	tick	trout
tarantula	tiger moth	tuna
Tasmanian devil	tiger salamander	turkey
Tasmanian tiger	tiger shark	turtle
tawny owl	toad	turtledove
tench	tortoise	
tern	toucan	
terrier	toy poodle	
thresher shark	tree frog	
thrush	triggerfish	

Get Creative I

accelerate	elude	obliterate
adore	empower	pester
appease	festoon	postpone
bicker	flout	rally
bulldoze	galvanize	saunter
burden	hone	smirk
captivate	humiliate	tarnish
censure	intrude	thrive
deteriorate	lament	thwart
dispel	mortify	undertake

Business As U-su-AL

animal	global	normal
arrival	gradual	oval
casual	herbal	plural
coral	individual	rival
decimal	local	rural
equal	mammal	several
factual	mineral	spiral
floral	moral	terminal
formal	mural	vertical
general	naval	virtual

Snap 'Em Up!

bag	grasp	secure
capture	grip	seize
catch	hold	snag
clasp	land	snap up
clench	latch on to	snare
cling	lay hold of	snatch
clutch	nab	take
get a hold of	nail	take hold of
grab	net	trap
grapple	pick up	wrest

Illegal To Irresponsible

illegal	inability	inhuman
illegible	inactive	inhumane
illiberal	incorrect	insecure
illiterate	indecisive	insoluble
illogical	indirect	invalid
immature	inedible	irrational
immortal	inequality	irregular
impatient	inexact	irrelevant
imperfect	inexplicable	irreparable
impossible	informal	irresponsible

Chic 'Ch'

brioche	chevron	parachute
cartouche	chic	pastiche
champagne	chiffon	pistachio
chandelier	chute	quiche
charade	cliché	ricochet
château	crochet	
chauffeur	gouache	
chef	machine	
chemise	Michigan	
chevalier	mustache	

King Arthur & Co.

Arthur	Arthurian	betrayal
Merlin	Camelot	chivalry
Guinevere	Avalon	gallantry
Lancelot	Excalibur	honor
Morgan le Fay	Round Table	romance
Lady of the Lake	giants	sword
Gawain	knights	joust
Galahad	ladies	lance
Bedivere	lords	quests
Modred	squires	tournaments

Joining Forces

afternoon	footprint	rainbow
backfire	haircut	skyscraper
bathroom	headhunter	sunbeam
cardboard	inkblot	sunset
caveman	keepsake	superpower
deadline	lighthouse	timetable
egghead	litterbug	toothbrush
everywhere	mainstream	touchdown
eyebrow	pinhole	underground
fingerprint	pothole	upstairs

Ex Marks The Spot!

excavate	context	annex
excellent	dexterous	apex
exclamation	dyslexia	complex
exercise	hexagon	convex
exhale	hypertext	flex
expert	lexicon	ibex
export	nexus	index
exterior	plexus	perplex
external	textile	vex
extra	texture	vortex

On Your Feet!

ankle boot	half boot	safety shoe
ballet slipper	high heels	sandal
clog	hobnail boot	slingback
combat boot	lace-up	slipper
cowboy boot	loafer	sneaker
espadrille	moccasin	snowshoe
flat	mule	stiletto
flip-flop	platform shoe	tennis shoe
galosh	pump	top boot
golf shoe	running shoe	Wellingtons

Grrr-ammar!

determiner	personal	past
noun	relative	present
verb	conjunction	future
modal verb	root	simple
adverb	prefix	progressive
adjective	suffix	perfect
comparative	adverbial	active
superlative	phrase	passive
preposition	clause	singular
pronoun	subordinate	plural

Game On!

backgammon	mah-jongg	snakes and ladders
Battleship	mancala	solitaire
checkers	Mastermind	Trivial Pursuit
chess	Monopoly	Twister
Chinese checkers	nine-men's morris	Yahtzee
Clue	Operation	
Connect 4	pachisi	
dominoes	Pictionary	
Go	Risk	
Jenga	Scrabble	

Making It

assemble	fashion	prepare
author	forge	produce
build	form	raise
compose	formulate	rear
construct	generate	shape
craft	invent	
create	manufacture	
design	model	
devise	mold	
fabricate	originate	

Silent, But Deadly II

calf	stalkless	folksy
calves	talk	kinfolk
half	talking	kinsfolk
halves	walk	colonel
halved	walker	salmon
behalf	jaywalk	
halfway	spacewalk	
chalk	could	
chalky	should	
stalk	folk	

As The Crow Flies

albatross	lark	seagull
chaffinch	magpie	sparrow
chough	moorhen	starling
emu	nightingale	woodpecker
flamingo	nightjar	wren
hummingbird	partridge	
jackdaw	peacock	
jay	pheasant	
kite	raven	
kiwi	rook	

Happy Endings II

advantageous	studious	notorious
courageous	various	oblivious
outrageous	victorious	obvious
beauteous	curious	odious
bounteous	delirious	previous
envious	devious	religious
furious	hilarious	serious
glorious	imperious	tedious
luxurious	ingenious	hideous
mysterious	luminous	courteous

FOURTH OF JULY

balloons	declaration	federal
banners	independence	free
bunting	patriotism	memorable
flags	proclamation	solemn
streamers	tradition	united
barbecues	celebrate	
baseball games	debate	
theme parks	observe	
parades	salute	
picnics	vote	

Double Trouble?

admitted	preferred	watered
admitting	preferring	watering
emitted	regretted	interpreted
emitting	regretting	interpreting
hammered	submitted	numbered
hammering	submitting	numbering
occurred	blanketed	opened
occurring	blanketing	opening
omitted	bordered	wandered
omitting	bordering	wandering

Tech Talk

blog	hit	podcaster
blogging	home page	search engine
bookmark	live stream	spam
broadband	meme	upload
browser	message board	URL
chat room	newsgroup	vlog
cookie	offline	web page
domain name	online	webcam
download	paywall	website
email	podcast	Wi-Fi

All Over The Place!

top	minus	beneath
bottom	within	beyond
beginning	without	during
middle	beside	into
end	next to	past
right	around	
left	round	
up	amid	
down	among	
plus	against	

Perfect? Prefect?

perceive	permanent	prelude
percentage	permit	premium
percussion	persist	preserve
performance	personify	president
perfume	persuade	prestige
perhaps	precise	presto
peril	predatory	pretense
perimeter	predict	prettify
periscope	preen	prevail
perish	prefer	prevent

Farmers Market

beet	leek	squash
broccoli	lettuce	sweet corn
brussels sprout	mushroom	turnip
cauliflower	parsley	yam
celery	parsnip	zucchini
chicory	radish	
chili	rocket	
coriander	rutabaga	
fennel	shallot	
kale	spring onion	

Get Creative II

ablaze	earnest	placid
arid	enduring	prickling
bedraggled	faultless	quaking
beloved	genial	shrouded
boisterous	glazed	threadbare
charismatic	mindless	tolling
convenient	monotonous	tumultuous
daring	noiseless	unflinching
decrepit	outspoken	woeful
deluxe	penniless	wondrous

Kingly 'K'

kangaroo	keystroke	kingfisher
karate	khaki	kingliness
karma	kickstand	kingmaker
kebab	kidnapper	kink
keen	kilogram	kiosk
keg	kilometer	kitchenware
kennel	kindle	koala
kerchief	kindness	kohl
kettledrum	kindred	kookaburra
keyboard	kinetic	kraken

C Is For Camel &...

camel	Chihuahua	cockroach
canary	chimpanzee	collie
caribou	chinchilla	condor
carp	chipmunk	copperhead
caterpillar	cicada	cormorant
catfish	civet	coyote
centipede	clam	crab
cheetah	clown fish	crane
chickadee	cobra	crow
chicken	cockatoo	cuttlefish

A...CHoo?

batch	stitch	stretchy
blotch	twitch	ditched
crutch	butcher	thatched
dispatch	catcher	wretched
etch	pitcher	hatchet
glitch	stretcher	ketchup
notch	watcher	kitchen
patch	catchy	satchel
sketch	itchy	watchful
snitch	scratchy	watchman

Hide & Seek!

hide	smuggle	fish for
bury	squirrel away	go after
camouflage	stash	hunt down
cloak	suppress	investigate
conceal	veil	nose out
disguise	seek	probe
entomb	chase	pursue
mask	comb	scrutinize
obscure	delve	search out
secrete	ferret out	track

Head-Scratchers

accept	fort	rain
except	fought	rein
affect	grate	war
effect	great	wore
bite	hoard	weather
byte	horde	whether
boar	law	who's
bore	lore	whose
farther	main	wood
father	mane	would

Fine And Handy!

Allen wrench
axe
bolt
chisel
clamp
crowbar
duct tape
flashlight
friction tape
hammer
hand drill
handsaw
ladder
mallet
nail
nut
paint roller
paintbrush
pincers
pliers
putty
sander
sandpaper
saw
screwdriver
spirit level
tape measure
toolbox
utility knife
wrench

Happy Endings III

accusation
admiration
adoration
aspiration
civilization
colonization
combination
condensation
configuration
conjuration
conversation
decoration
determination
dispensation
dramatization
examination
exploration
imagination
improvisation
inclination
inspiration
intonation
modernization
organization
perspiration
preparation
restoration
sensation
synchronization
transfiguration

Sweet Tooth

apple dumpling	Danish pastry	muffin
angel food cake	devil's food cake	pancake
baklava	doughnut	panettone
Black Forest cake	éclair	pavlova
brownie	flapjack	profiterole
cannoli	frangipane	scone
cheesecake	fruitcake	stollen
coffee ring	gingerbread	tarte tatin
cream puff	key lime pie	tiramisu
cupcake	macaroon	trifle

Plague? Plaque?

ague	plague	clique
colleague	prologue	critique
dialogue	rogue	grotesque
epilogue	vague	masque
fatigue	vogue	mystique
intrigue	antique	opaque
league	arabesque	physique
monologue	baroque	plaque
morgue	bisque	technique
oblique	boutique	unique

Happy Days!

after-party	festival	jubilee
anniversary	festivity	masquerade
ball	fete	pageant
birthday	fiesta	parade
carnival	function	party
cavalcade	gala	procession
celebration	graduation	prom
centennial	holy day	reception
costume party	housewarming	reunion
dance	jamboree	soiree

Something Fishy

barnacle	manatee	sea urchin
barracuda	manta ray	seahorse
coral reef	mussel	seal
dolphin	narwhal	shrimp
dugong	octopus	squid
hermit crab	oyster	starfish
jellyfish	plankton	stingray
limpet	porpoise	swordfish
lobster	prawn	walrus
mackerel	sardine	whale

OH MY, OH Y

ally	encyclopedia	rhyme
apply	hydrogen	rye
bypass	hygiene	sly
cyberspace	hype	spry
cycle	hyphen	spy
cypress	ply	style
defy	pry	thyme
deny	pylon	type
dye	python	typhoon
dynamic	reply	tyrant

Glug, Glug, Glug

belt down	knock back	swallow
chug	lap	swig
consume	partake of	swill
down	polish off	toss back
drain	quaff	wash down
drink	sip	
drink up	slug down	
gulp	slurp	
guzzle	suck	
imbibe	sup	

Confounded Conjunctions

after	neither	whenever
although	nor	where
and	once	wherever
as	or	while
because	since	yet
before	so	
but	that	
for	unless	
how	until	
if	when	

Written In The Stars

Aries	Aquarius	destiny
Taurus	Pisces	fate
Gemini	horoscope	personality
Cancer	star sign	potential
Leo	zodiac	strengths
Virgo	astrologer	traits
Libra	astrology	weaknesses
Scorpio	celestial	planets
Sagittarius	chart	lunar
Capricorn	constellation	solar

What's A Person Who...

antiquarian	guardian	theologian
beautician	humanitarian	thespian
civilian	librarian	totalitarian
comedian	parliamentarian	vegetarian
custodian	patrician	veterinarian
dietitian	pedestrian	
disciplinarian	pediatrician	
documentarian	statistician	
equestrian	tactician	
grammarian	technician	

Silent, But Deadly III

apostle	thistle	soften
bristle	trestle	ballet
bustle	whistle	beret
castle	wrestle	chalet
epistle	christen	croquet
gristle	fasten	duvet
jostle	glisten	gourmet
nestle	hasten	mistletoe
pestle	listen	mortgage
rustle	moisten	rapport

WHERE IN THE WORLD...?

Alexandria	Khartoum	Rio de Janeiro
Bangkok	Kinshasa	Riyadh
Beijing	Lagos	San Diego
Delhi	Lahore	São Paulo
Dhaka	Lima	Seoul
Houston	Madrid	Shanghai
Istanbul	Manila	Singapore
Jakarta	Mexico City	Tehran
Johannesburg	Moscow	Tokyo
Karachi	Paris	Toronto

Colorific!

attractive	gentle	tinted
bleached	neutral	vibrant
bold	painted	vivid
brilliant	pale	washed-out
colorful	pastel	watery
deep	rich	
dyed	shaded	
electric	soft	
eye-catching	striking	
faint	tinged	

Are You Sure...Or Ture?

closure	indenture	restructure
composure	juncture	rupture
displeasure	legislature	scripture
enclosure	mixture	suture
exposure	moisture	tincture
agriculture	nurture	
architecture	pasture	
denture	posture	
fixture	puncture	
horticulture	recapture	

FULL OF BEANS!

adzuki bean	green bean	string bean
black bean	jack bean	tonka bean
borlotti	kidney bean	white bean
broad bean	moth bean	winged bean
butter bean	mung bean	yard-long bean
cannellini bean	navy bean	
dwarf bean	pinto bean	
edamame	red bean	
flageolet	scarlet runner bean	
great northern bean	soybean	

Sssss...

censorship	cilantro	furnace
census	cinder	palace
cent	cinema	space
centaur	cinnamon	notice
center	cipher	office
centerpiece	citadel	flounce
centigrade	citizen	silence
centimeter	citrus	commerce
centurion	city	force
century	civil	source

Lots 'N Lots 'N Lots

keyboards	princesses	appendixes
posters	armies	boxes
railings	candies	foxes
sidewalks	trophies	ibexes
windows	elves	taxes
bicycles	hooves	cacti
cobblestones	loaves	fungi
engines	wolves	indices
compasses	echoes	analyses
dresses	mosquitoes	geese

By Jupiter!

Diana	aqueduct	chariot
Dis	Colosseum	fresco
Juno	forum	mosaic
Jupiter	temple	toga
Mars	triumphal arch	tunic
Mercury	consul	engineering
Minerva	magistrate	history
Neptune	plebeian	philosophy
Venus	senator	poetry
Vulcan	tribune	rhetoric

Clippety-Clop, Clippety-Clop

bound	gallop	skip
canter	glide	skitter
crawl	hop	slither
creep	leap	soar
dive	lollop	stampede
dogtrot	lope	strut
flap	prance	swoop
flit	prowl	trot
flutter	scamper	waddle
fly	scuttle	wriggle

Antihero Or Superstar?

antibiotic
antibody
antidote
antihero
antiperspirant
antiseptic
autobiography
autocorrect
autograph
automatic

autopilot
autosave
interchange
interject
interlude
international
interrupt
intersect
subdivide
subheading

submarine
submerge
submerse
subset
superbug
superimpose
superman
supermarket
superscript
superstar

Knock On Wood

ash
aspen
balsa
banyan
beech
birch
cedar
ebony
elm
fir

hardwood
hazel
hickory
larch
mahogany
mangrove
maple
oak
pine
poplar

red cedar
red fir
rosewood
sandalwood
spruce
sycamore
teak
walnut
willow
yew

Happy Endings IV

clinician	erosion	suspension
magician	evasion	tension
optician	fusion	admission
physician	infusion	commission
politician	intrusion	confession
aversion	persuasion	discussion
collision	precision	expression
corrosion	profusion	impression
delusion	protrusion	possession
diversion	provision	submission

Chowin' Down

appetizer	cookout	Oslo breakfast
banquet	dinner	picnic
barbecue	dinner party	potluck
box lunch	English breakfast	shore dinner
breakfast	feast	smorgasbord
brunch	fish fry	supper
buffet	high tea	tailgate party
clambake	luau	tapas
coffee break	lunch	TV dinner
Continental breakfast	luncheon	working breakfast

It's All Make-Believe...

chimeric	fantastic	legendary
chimerical	fantastical	made-up
concocted	fictional	make-believe
dreamed up	fictitious	mythic
dreamlike	fictive	mythical
fabled	ideal	mythological
fabricated	illusory	nonexistent
fabulous	imaginary	phantom
fanciful	imagined	pretend
fantasied	invented	unreal

The Real Deal

accurate	incontestable	real
actual	incontrovertible	recognizable
authentic	indisputable	substantiated
bona fide	irrefutable	undeniable
certain	lawful	undoubted
certified	legal	unmistakable
established	legitimate	unquestionable
genuine	original	validated
guaranteed	proper	verifiable
identifiable	proven	verified

What A Ra-CK-et!

background	racket	hammock
beckon	sickle	hemlock
bracket	socket	hijack
cricket	speckled	maverick
cuckoo	tacky	padlock
gecko	aback	paperback
jackal	attack	ransack
jockey	flock	shipwreck
mockery	gimmick	sundeck
necklace	gridlock	thwack

Heads First

archduke	king	raja
caliph	maharaja	rani
czar	maharani	satrap
doge	mikado	shah
duke	nabob	sheikh
emir	nawab	shogun
emperor	oba	stadtholder
empress	pasha	sultan
khan	pope	vicereine
khedive	queen	viceroy

...Er

coroner	anger	conquer
hacker	answer	deliver
hiker	laughter	flicker
jeweler	power	prosper
juggler	semester	register
officer	bitter	surrender
partner	clever	swagger
trader	sinister	trigger
usher	slender	whimper
worker	tender	whisper

D Is For Disaster

annihilation	demolition	obliteration
apocalypse	destruction	ruin
Armageddon	devastation	tragedy
bloodbath	doomsday	upheaval
calamity	havoc	wreckage
carnage	loss	
catastrophe	meltdown	
collapse	mischance	
debacle	misfortune	
decimation	mishap	

Write On!

advice columnist
biographer
blogger
columnist
diarist
dramatist
editor
essayist
ghostwriter
historian
humorist
journalist
letter writer
librettist
lyricist
novelist
philosopher
playwright
poet
reporter
satirist
screenwriter
scribe
scriptwriter
tweeter

Clouding Over

ashen
bleak
clouded
colorless
darkened
darkish
dim
dismal
drab
dreary
dull
dusky
eclipsed
faded
foggy
gloomy
leaden
lightless
misty
moonless
murky
muted
overcast
shadowy
smoggy
somber
soupy
starless
sunless
unilluminated

V..V.. VAMPIRES!

alluring	horror	silver
coffin	invitation	stake
consecrated	legend	stamina
crucifix	malevolent	sunlight
crypt	menacing	supernatural
Dracula	mirror	superstition
fangs	nocturnal	terror
folklore	paranormal	threshold
garlic	predator	Transylvania
graveyard	reflection	undead

THAT'S A PROPER WORD?!

aplomb	jetsam	umlaut
diddly-squat	kibosh	windbag
doodad	moonstruck	wiseacre
egad	mudslinging	wombat
flotsam	pell-mell	yokel
frippery	quibble	
gasbag	rapscallion	
glad rags	sassafras	
helter-skelter	slapdash	
humdrum	slipshod	

INDEX

In the following entries, the letter 'A' refers to the upper list on the page, while 'B' refers to the lower one.

ELA WORDS

Commonly Mistaken Spellings (p. 8: B)

Compound Words (p. 12: B)

Conjunctions (p. 27: A)

Doubling Consonants or Not with Suffixes (p. 17: B)

Homophones & Near Homophones (p. 22: B)

Key Grammar Terms (p. 14: A)

Letter Sounds
  ce or ci as 's' (p. 31: A)
  ch as 'sh' (p. 11: B)
  ou as 'ow' (p. 8: A)
  y as 'long i' (p. 26: A)

Letter Strings
  Words beginning with non-silent 'k' (p. 20: B)
  Words beginning with 'per' or 'pre' (p. 19: A)
  Words containing 'ck' (p. 36: A)
  Words containing 'ex' (p. 13: A)
  Words containing 'tch' (p. 21: B)
  Words ending in 'al' (p. 10: A)
  Words ending in 'er' (p. 37: A)
  Words ending in 'gue' & 'que' (p. 24: B)
  Words ending in 'sure' & 'ture' (p. 30: A)

Plural Nouns (p. 31: B)

Prefixes
  anti- auto- inter- sub- & super- (p. 33: A)
  il- im- in- & ir- (p. 11: A)
  mis- (p. 7: A)

Silent Letters
  Silent 'g' (p. 6: A)
  Silent 'l' (p. 15: B)
  Silent 't' (p. 28: B)

Suffixes
  -ation (p. 23: B)
  -ian -sion & -ssion (p. 34: A)
  -ly (p. 5: A)
  -ous & -ious (p. 16: B)

GENERAL KNOWLEDGE WORDS

Ancient Rome (p. 32: A)
Astrology (p. 27: B)
Beans, Types of (p. 30: B)
Birds (p. 16: A)
Board & Card Games (p. 14: B)
Cakes & Pastries (p. 24: A)
Cities of the World (p. 29: A)
Creatures starting with C (p. 21: A)
Creatures starting with T (p. 9: A)
Footwear (p. 13: B)
Fourth of July (p. 17: A)
Fresh Produce (p. 19: B)
Happy Occasions (p. 25: A)
Internet, The (p. 18: A)
King Arthur (p. 12: A)
Marine Life (p. 25: B)
Meals, Types of (p. 34: B)
Rulers, Types of (p. 36: B)
Tools (p. 23: A)
Types of People: -ian ending (p. 28: A)
Types of People: -or ending (p. 7: B)
Vampires (p. 39: A)
Wood & Trees, Types of (p. 33: B)
Writers, Types of (p. 38: A)

ANTONYM PAIR
Hide vs. Seek (p. 22: A)

SYNONYMS

Adjectives
Imaginary (p. 35: A)
Real (p. 35: B)

Verbs
Change (p. 6: B)
Cheat (p. 5: B)
Drink (p. 26: B)
Make (p. 15: A)
Take (hold of) (p. 10: B)

WORD CLUSTERS
Color-related Words (p. 29: B)
Creatures' Movements (p. 32: B)
Disasters (p. 37: B)
Dim Lighting Words (p. 38: B)
Place & Position Words (p. 18: B)

CREATIVE WRITING WORDS

Fun Words (p. 39: B)

Powerful Adjectives (p. 20: A)

Powerful Verbs (p. 9: B)